FORGIVE ME FORGIVE ME NOT

VOL 4

PAMELA TUCKER

Copyright © 2020 By Pamela Tucker

All rights reserved. No part of this publication may be reproduced, distributed, or transmitted in any form or by any means, including photocopying, recording, or other electronic or mechanical methods, without the prior written permission of the publisher, except in the case of brief quotations embodied in critical reviews and certain other non-commercial uses permitted by copyright law. For permission requests, write to the publisher, addressed, "Attention: Permissions Coordinator" at the address below.

Printed in the United States Of America

First printing, 2020

ISBN: 978-1-7350031-2-2

Email: ReStartenterprise2017@gmail.com

All Scripture references are taken from the New King James Version unless otherwise stated.

Acknowledgments

I thank God for His grace, mercy, and strength to complete these chapters of my life. Without Him, none of these would have been possible. I thank God for my beautiful family. He's blessed me with 3 beautiful daughters, Olivia, Antiea, Breanna, and my precious granddaughter, Peyton. I appreciate the immense care and support from my siblings, Mary, Jimmy, and Brenda, as well as my friends.

Thank you all for your encouragement,Love, support, push and your prayers.

I Love You All.

Table Of Contents

Chapter One: You Don't Know Him 1

Chapter Two: It Took Years To Be Free 23

Chapter Three: The Day I Stood Still 47

Chapter Four: Poem I'm Free 50

Chapter Five: I Will Not 54

Chapter Six: Encourage Yourself With The I Am's. 56

Bible Scriptures 62

The Sinner's Prayer 66

A Prayer For You 68

About The Author 70

CHAPTER ONE

YOU DON'T KNOW HIM

"Why are you lying to me? I don't believe anything you are saying; you will leave my house. I don't care where you go. Just get out of here. You need some help. You need to find somewhere else to live," Karen gushed.

"Where am I going to go, mom? I am your child," Chelsea retorted.

"You are not my child lying to me."

"I'm not lying. Please mom, help me, and hear me."

"I don't have time for you. I can't help, nor do I want to hear you. I am going to get you out of my house."

"Mom, who are you calling? Please, don't call the police. They will take me away and I will never see you again. Okay, mom, I was just lying because I don't want you to marry him. Who is he mom?" Chelsea said, "Mom you don't know Rodney."

"You wasted my time with these lies all because you don't want me to marry Rodney? Yea, you are leaving my house until Rodney and I get married."

Karen picked up the phone, "Hey Arianna, can you get Chelsea for a little while, Honey? She told lies about Rodney. I can't even talk about it now. She just got to go. She can't stay here right now. So, can you come and get her?"

"Karen, you know Chelsea should not be leaving her house because of a man. He should not be staying there no way then that would not be a problem. He hasn't touched Chelsea, has he?

"No, it's nothing like that. She just doesn't want us getting married," Karen reported.

"I told you, don't play house with that man, and I don't think you should marry him." "Well, Ariana, I don't need to hear a speech from you again about, 'This is not right in the eyes of God, and what God said.' I did not ask you about any of that.

"Karen, what happened to you? You used to walk so close to God, so faithful to God. The Karen I knew would never let a man come between her and her daughter. Karen, you were so bright and kind, beautiful, and smart. You own your things, house, car, and businesses. Now you took out loans on something you already paid off.

It doesn't make sense, Karen. Why are you letting this man bewitch you?" Rodney is a con artist and manipulator.

I don't care if he is a leader in his church, something is not right with him .

Arianna, all I would like to know if you can take

this trouble maker off my hands.

Karen, you know that God is not pleased with this. He gave you Chelsea. You remember how hard it was when you and your first husband wanted a baby and you all prayed, I prayed, and the church prayed with you all. Eventually, God answered and gave you a beautiful baby girl. You called her your God-sent girl. But now you call her a trouble maker and try to put her out of her house all because of a man? That's not right.

"Okay, thank you for the speech, and the walk down memory lane, but that was 11 years ago and Chelsea's dad is dead. Arianna, there is too much happening in the world today. I want to be married again before this world ends. I want to have a good life and be happy. I know you are going to say that Jesus can make you happy. I don't want to hear any of that right now. I am getting ready to get married and I have a lot of things I need to do. So, can you please come to get her, Arianna?"

"Karen, Rodney is nothing like your husband,

Mark, And if you are looking for a replacement for Mark, Rodney is not it .

"Okay Arianna, can you pick her up or not? Karen asked with an air of finalism.

"Where is your car, Karen?"

"Oh um um, Rodney had to take care of something," she excused.

"Yeah, okay. I will come to pick up Chelsea.

I am praying for you, Karen because this is not like you.

"Great, she will be ready." "Chelsea!" She yelled, "Get your clothes, you are going to stay with Auntie for a while."

I didn't say anything. I just got my clothes. I was glad to be going over auntie Arianna's house. She always listens to me. My Mom and she have been best friends since 1st grade, and people thought they were sisters. When Auntie came, she said we are going to do girls' night. If you would like to be sure, I replied, "So let us go to the store and get items for our girls' night." I was happy to be with my aunt. So we went into the store and got all kinds of items and goodies snacks.

When we got to Auntie's house, we pulled into the garage and started taking everything into the house. She said, "it is still the way you left it," with a big grin on her face. She said everything will be okay. I gave her a big hug. For some reasons, I believed her. I took my things to the room I have at her house. I went in, and everything was just the way I left it, one sock on the floor, the other on the bed. It felt so relaxing just to be back in my room at my auntie's house. I could not help but think about my mom and that man. I shook myself out of the thoughts that were playing in my head. I heard my auntie calling me asking me if everything was okay. "Yes auntie, everything is good. I am putting away my clothes."

When I came downstairs, I could hear Auntie on the phone with my mom. She was asking her why she was marrying this man. My mom said it's because he loves her."

"Really, Karen, He doesn't love you. Do you love him?" My mom never answered that question .

"Arianna, I can't talk right now. Rodney is coming into the house. I have to go.

"You can't even talk when he comes into the house? He is a control freak, a bully, a user, Karen. Can't you see this? You have never spoken to your daughter like that until you started fooling with him. I don't tell me he is going to change, you are not God .

He has the devil inside of him that he doesn't know what to change. He tells you stuff and treats you mean and that's making you act like this toward Chelsea, your family and your friends. We love you. That man doesn't love you, Karen.

Arianna, I got to go, bye.

I came down like I didn't hear anything, "Auntie, what's for lunch?" She said, "Would you like to cook?

"Hmmm, I will make some mini fish subs, and mini chicken subs."

"Yummy, sounds good. Get to the cooking, and I will set everything up on lanai," she said. So we went about our duties.

I had everything so beautiful. I want it to be a great setting for Chelsea and me to talk about her mom and Rodney. Everything was looking good and smelling so great. I went into the kitchen to check on Chelsea. She was still cooking and everything looked and smelled so good. She and I started to bring the food out on the lanai. She stepped out to the lanai, and it said, "welcome back." She was taken unaware, "Wow auntie, you really know how to make me feel special," she said. "That's because you are special," I replied.

At that moment, her face changed. She looked kind of sad. "What's wrong sweetie?

"Nothing, auntie. I'm just happy to be here."

I replied, "Okay, great, let us eat. After lunch, I will make us some lemon and grapefruit ices. Lest I forget, Chelsea, these mini-subs are delicious."

In the midst of our eating, Chelsea wanted to share something with me. I said, "Sure, sweetie. What is it?" I said, while taking my last bite. She said that she had a friend that had been made to do something that she did not like but she doesn't have anyone to tell it to. I said, "Tell me what your friend has been made to do." With a puzzling look on her face, she said, "She was made to wait for auntie's famous lemon grapefruit ices," then she smiled. She truly got me there. I said, "Sweetie, you know you had my attention." She said, "Yeah, I know that was funny."

I felt like Chelsea needed to share something with me but she is trying to fill me out to see how I am going to handle it. I'm going to be patient with her and let her tell me when she gets ready. I fixed my famous ices. She liked them.

"Auntie, can we watch a movie?"

"Yes, sure, but after we go walking on the track"

"Okay, great," Chelsea said.

"It's lovely out here looking at the birds and butterflies, feel that air blow on you. Thank you, Jesus."

Chelsea said, "Auntie, you thank God for everything."

I said, "Yep, I do. He tells us to give Him thanks in all things."

"But how can you thank Him for your pain?" Chelsea questioned.

"I thank Him because He said in all things to give thanks. It also let me know that I am still among the living," I answered.

So Chelsea said something that got me lost for a moment. She said, "How can you thank God for being touched in the wrong way?"

I said, "What do you mean touched?

"Auntie, Rodney has been touching me."

I was taken aback, and asked, "Touching you sexually?"

She said, "Yes auntie," and the story began. She told me what he would do to her. She said "I tried to tell my mom, but she told me that I was lying. She did not believe me and she told me that I needed to get out of her house. Why did my mom take up from him? I was telling her the truth."

Oh, I could feel her pain as she told me what he did to her. The more she told me, the angrier I got. When she was finished, we both were silent in tears, sobbing. When I hugged Chelsea, she broke out with a yell, "What did I do wrong?"

She told me everything started when she was 10 years old. She said that Rodney would come over to the house to see her mom. One day, her mom was not there, and "He said my mom told him to wait inside if he got to the house before she did. So I let him come in. He sat down on the sofa and said 'You look just like your mom but you are a lot prettier.' I did not say anything. I didn't feel alright around him. I was hoping my mom would come home quickly. He said, 'Chelsea, what are you doing?' I said, 'My homework.' He said, 'You need help?' 'No sir,' I replied. He said, 'What is your worst subject?' I told him Spanish. He started saying words in Spanish. I was like, oh you know how to speak Spanish. He said, 'Chelsea, if you need some help, I can help you.'

Auntie, I was happy to hear that because I was failing in that class. So he told me to repeat after him, 'si me ayudas te ayudare.' I said, 'What does that mean?' He said it means 'If you help me, I will help you.' I said, 'Help you do what?' He said, 'I will let you know when the time comes. I just want to help you pass that class,' with a big grin on his face. At that time, my mom came in and greeted him with a big hug all on him. Then she said to me, 'Chelsea, you did your homework yet?' 'Yes, mom, I am working on it now. Rodney said he could help me with my Spanish.' He said,

'Yeah baby, I will help the child out.' My mom said he was so nice and so smart he knew 5 different languages."

I asked her, "Chelsea, did you tell your mom?" She said, "I tried to tell her on a few different occasions."

"And what did she say?"

"Nothing, or she would say that I am lying. Then Rodney would come over late in the evening and tell my mom he is helping me with my Spanish. She would say yes to anything for him. She loves him more than she loves me. So, he would start naming body parts that I can understand. He then would say it in Spanish. I gave him a list of words that I had to learn in Spanish, not the ones he was saying. He said I had to learn his own words first, then he will help me with the other words for my homework. He would say inappropriate words to me then he would say them in Spanish. It started out like that. He would say the word and touch me in the place. I knew he should have not begun touching me.

He started rubbing, kissing, and fondling me. He was showing me pictures of all kinds of bad stuff. Auntie, he said that he can do anything to me because I was black and he was white. The way he looked at me I got so scared. I knew I had to make mom believe me, but when she started talking about sending me away, I got scared even more because of what Rodney said could happen. So, I told her I was just playing. Then she called you auntie. I am so nervous that something is going to happen to me."

I held her close and tried to reassure her, "Sweetie, don't be nervous. We will take care of this but first, we have to pray." We prayed for forgiveness, understanding, healing, love, wisdom, and direction in this matter. After we prayed, I told Chelsea what we had to do was to call her mom and tell her again, and this time she will believe her. Chelsea still doesn't want to tell her mom because her mom was so in love with Rodney and she might take his word over hers again. "She already did it before. That's why I am here with you, auntie." I just hugged her. She was so hurt. How could her mom treat her like that because of a man?

"Chelsea, we have to call your mom now." She said, "Okay auntie, if you think so." I rang her, "Hey, Karen, we need to talk." She said, "I was just going to call you. How is Chelsea?" She's okay; she's concerned about you, Karen. I will be on my way when the police leave." I replied, "Police? Karen are you okay?" "Yes, I will explain when I get there," She said, and we hung up. Chelsea asked me if everything was okay with her mom. "She's coming over; she said she needs to talk." Chelsea asked, "Did she sound mad, auntie?" I answered, "No sweetie, she didn't."

After a few hours, Karen rang the doorbell, and we got the door. Karen came in and asked if we can talk upstairs in my prayer room. "Yes, sure," I replied. So, we went up and sat on the prayer pillows. Karen did not say anything for a moment. When she spoke, she said, "Chelsea, you are my God-sent girl, and I am asking you to please forgive me." Chelsea said, "Mom, I forgive you." They hugged and cried together.

Karen said, "I believed you the first time, but I was scared. I am not even sure why I was scared, but in the night, I began to have doubts about marrying him. So I told him, and he got angry. I went to the prayer closet and locked the door. He banged and banged to no avail. Then he got my keys and sped off in my car. I came out and called the police on him because of what he said he would do to me. You told me what Rodney was doing. I just could not believe he could do something like that to you."

I was in denial, and interrupted her, "We hear you Karen, but what happened today?"

"Today, a woman and a young girl came to my door. She said, 'My name is Lolonyo, and my daughter is Zuri. We would like to speak to you about Rodney.'

I was thinking that the woman was going to

say that she was his wife and that's his daughter. So I said, 'Sure come on in and have a seat.'

As they sat down, she said, 'I will not beat around the brush. I followed Rodney one day to this house, and I saw you outside.' She said she was not going to say anything but something would not let her rest. So that's why she was here. She said, 'I don't think you know who Rodney really is. I met Rodney at my daughter's school. He was a part-time counselor at the school and my daughter was having some problems with some school bullies. So she was assigned to Rodney for counseling to help her cope with being in a new school and a different country without her father. So I met Mr. Rodney in his office and he told me he could help Zuri and I shouldn't worry about anything. The first few weeks, everything was fine. It seemed like he was helping Zuri and she was happy she had friends and everything was going good. Next thing I knew, Zuri was like she was afraid to go to school. Long story short, he had told Zuri not to say anything or else they will take her away from me and she wouldn't have a father nor a mother. He said it is because he is a white man and she is a black girl. He showed her pictures of himself, and he would touch her in an inappropriate way. He would say nasty words to her. I had him arrested. He's out of the school and he can't hurt any more kids.'

I was sitting looking like a deer in headlights. I could not move nor speak; I was shocked. She said, 'I am not sure if you have a daughter. If so, you might need to ask her some questions because he has been doing this for years. He is wanted in 4 other states for the same thing. I put a camera on Zuri's clothes to find out what was going on at school. I was thinking it was the bullies again. Can you imagine how I felt looking at him touching my daughter like that? Everything that has happened, my daughter doesn't really talk. We have taken up enough of your time. I wanted you to know the truth about Rodney.'

I said I'm so sorry for what they all had been

through. She said, 'It is not your fault.' I promised I will be praying for them both. I also told Lolonyo if I could do anything she should please let me know. We exchanged phone numbers.

It was so much that Lolonyo shared with me, just too much to tell everything right now, but Rodney has to go to court in those other states. After they left, I called to see if her story was true. It turned out everything was true, plus more changes.

I told them he stayed with me, and I needed to know my rights. I want to change my phone number so he cannot call me again. They said I can do that. The police had to come and search the house for anything that could be evidence. They found some personal videotapes and some pictures all hidden in a big bag in the garage. They asked me if I knew that this was in the plant soil. I told them no, Rodney told me he was going to plant some flowers around the trees to enhance the yard. They asked me a lot of questions. They may have to ask you some questions Chelsea. I'm sorry baby; I should have listened to you. They said they will call me if they have to speak to you; they would send someone to the house.

Arianna, I am sorry that I didn't listen, and I know I said some hurtful words. Please forgive me."

I replied, "Karen, I forgive you. You are blessed; things could have been worse." Karen agreed.

Karen asked God to forgive her. She was repenting unto God, crying out for help. Chelsea had fallen asleep. Karen woke her up telling her to get in the bed. She said, "Yes mama." As she was walking out, she turned and said, "Mom, I love you. It is going to be okay." I love you auntie, goodnight y'all." We responded, "we love you too sweetie." Went back to praying and worshipping God. Once we were finished Karen said to me, "Arianna, I thought about what you shared with me about what happened to you when you were a young girl. I listened to you but I could not really relate because I never experienced anything like that."

I replied, "I know you could not, but you were there to listen to me and that helped me a lot. I guess that's why I could feel Chelsea's pain, hurt, disappointments, embarrassment , and shame when she was sharing things with me.

She will have to share it with you now that things are changing with you two. When she does tell you what happened, please just listen and love her through this with prayer, compassion, and truth. It's not easy having a mom that doesn't believe you. I never told her, but I truly believe my mom knew because she became more protective of me even when I got grown.

It is late Karen, get some rest." She said, "Thank you, my sister and friend. I love you Arianna." "I love you too Karen. We are family. Goodnight

I went into my room. Karen went into the guest room like she does when she comes over. When

I went into my room, I sat on my bed, and my mind began to play what had happened to me when I was a child.

CHAPTER TWO

IT TOOK YEARS TO BE FREE

I remember one beautiful day as a kid in the suburban neighborhood. The breeze was gentle and the sun was a template. My mom and sister had gone to the store. I was asleep when they left and my dad was watching me until they came back.. He was on the phone talking business when I woke up from my nap. I was ready to play.

I wanted to play with some kids, but I knew I could not go to one family that stayed on the left side of our house because the reputation was that they were into some things that were not good. I remember the first and last time I went over to their house. It was their dad and mom and six children that stayed in that house two of them were around my age. I was playing with the ones around my age ,one was 8 yrs the other was 10 years and I was 9years old. We were playing outside like kids do . The next thing I knew their dad came to the door and told them they had to get dressed. They asked me to wait for them to come back and I said okay sure". While I was waiting for them, my mom came over there to let me know that it was time to come home, by the time got ready to let them know I had to leave they came out with their faces half balck, white and red when my mom saw that she started speaking in another language and said come on Arianna she grabbed my hand and went walking fast toward home . When we got home she said don't go over there anymore. I didn't even ask why I was afraid of their faces, so I said yes ma'am.

All I knew was that the whole family would paint one side of their faces black ,red and , white when they played in a rock band.

So I knew going over there was out of the

question. I rode my big wheel in my backyard after awhile I got tired of playing by myself. I wanted to go to the other neighbors house next door to us to see if Connor could come out and play. I went back into my house and asked my dad if I could go next door to see if Connor could come out and play with me. My dad, still on the phone, shook his head in affirmation. So, off I went next door to go see if he was home, thinking to myself, "Connor and I could race our big wheels like we do sometimes."

We would play together at each other's house sometimes , we would play racing games, But most of the time we were outside. My mom did not let me go into their house a lot. I used to hear my dad and my uncles say that blacks and whites did not get along. I never believed it because my god-parents were white.

Also,I was a 9-year-old black girl, and was a friend to a 9-year-old white boy with red hair. His family lived next door.

His family seemed to like me. His dad, mom,

grandad lived there under one roof. On my way to their house my eyes peered up to the sky, where I took notice of the clouds. I loved how they were so full and fluffy. They were like huge cotton balls. I stared at each cloud and deciphered what each one was. It was fun for me to guess what animal or person that each cloud resembled. I was so happy that day.

Yes, today is a perfectly beautiful day.

I skipped my way over to see if Connor could come out and play. I knocked on the door like we always did and his granddad came to the door.

"Hi there Arianna, looking for Connor?"

I said, "Yes sir."

"He's in the back part of the house playing with his new train set. You can go on back."

I said, "Ok, thank you," and skipped on in.

I was not afraid I did this before Connor's granddad would say sometimes when Connor got new toys. I had been to their house before. I went into the back room where we had played many times. We built a train track set together one time.

When I got into the room, there was no sign of Connor nor train set. Granddad said, "Oh, he went to the store to get some toys."

I said, "Ok," and started toward the front door to go back home. Connor's granddad stood in front of the door, grabbed my arm, and told me to come with him.

"I want to show you something," he said

I whined, "No! I have to get home. My mom will be looking for me."

He retorted, "No. She left with your eldest sister." He took me to another room and told me he just wanted to kiss my chocolate skin.

I was tomboyish with a dress on and my mother did not buy me pants. I played in dresses. I did not understand why he wanted to do me like that.

I told him I wanted my mom, and I needed to

go home. He held me down on the bed and told me not to say anything, and if I did, my family would not see me anymore, because I was a black girl and he was a white man.

Wow, I could not understand why me. What did I do wrong?

"Please don't touch me. Please let me go!"

He put his hand over my mouth and put his hand under my dress. He touched my private with his finger. I was moving and crying; trying to yell, but he had his hand over my mouth. I was so scared. Tears rolled down my face. I was crying so hard that I felt like I could hardly breathe. He had his hand over my mouth and nose so tight. He told me I would not see my family if I tried to scream again or if I kept moving. He said he was going to move his hand from my mouth.

I said, "Please stop. I'm sorry. Please let me go. What did I do wrong?"

I kept apologizing and begging, "Please you are hurting me. Please stop! Help me please."

I cried out for my daddy.

"Help me, please daddy!" I yelled

He spewed obnoxious words to me then he started saying "SHUT UP." He started to shake me by the shoulders.

"Shut up or I will kill you."

I was so afraid. I said softly, "Help me, Lord!"

My driveway was right next to the room. A car was coming up and I tried to get up, but he would not let me. I knew it had to be my mom. It was my mom and sister coming home, I thought.

I pleaded again, "Please, my mom is coming to look for me, and she will know that I am here."

He looked at me. Then he got up and started to talk to himself about what he should do. He said again to himself frantically muttered to himself." "If I let her go, but no…" I can't, he said. He was talking and pacing back and forth to himself.

I was still crying—sniffling.

"Shut up girl. Stop crying." I can not think he said

He threatened that if I ever told anyone he would take me away from my family.

"I won't. Please let me go."

He let me get up. I pulled my panties up and he told me to look him in his face. He said that if I say anything that I would come up missing. He said because I was a black girl, I could come up missing and nobody would care, because he was a white man.

He opened the door and I was gone running fast to my house. I went in, my dad was still on the phone, I hid under the bed in the dark.

I was so scared I could not say anything to anyone. I just let the tears roll down my face while I hid under the bed—scared, hurting, crying, nervous, confused, and sad. All I could hear was his voice that bellowed in my ear drums. He could take me away from my family if I tell anyone. I was trying to stop crying before my mom or my sister came into the room. I heard the car, didn't I?

I stayed under the bed in a fetal position until I cried myself to sleep. When I woke up, my eldest sister was calling for me "Arianna "Arianna jay.

I came out, and she asked me, "Where were you?"

"Under the bed." I sheepishly replied . " I fell asleep," I answered.

My eldest sister was like my second mom. She always bought clothes, toys, and she was concerned about my wellbeing.

She was staring at me with a perplexed look on her face. It looks like

"You've been crying Arianna. What's wrong?" her voice was filled with such concern. I wanted so deeply to tell her, but I knew that I couldn't.

So I told her I did not feel good.

"What's hurting you?"

"I just don't feel well."

"I brought you something. Go try to eat something; maybe you will feel better."

I asked her, "Why did y'all leave me here?"

"You were asleep when mom and I left, so we let you sleep. Daddy was here watching you. Were you sleeping all this time?"

"I just don't feel good," I said, afraid to tell her. I tried to think of something to say. She checked me for a fever. She said I was just a little warm. She asked what was hurting me, and I said my stomach.

"I will run you some bathwater with lots of bubbles for you."

"Okay." I really like bubble baths.

When I got in the tub, my private area was hurting and burning very bad. I jumped out of the tub and told my mom how my private was feeling.

" Arianna, this is why I tell you to wipe properly when you tinkle.

The bath water will help you," she suggested.

I wanted to tell my mom what had happened, but If I told her, I wouldn't see my mom. I love my mom and my family, but if I told her I would not see them anymore. I just said "Okay," and got back in the tub. Wish I could tell my mom.

***

The next couple of days, I stayed in the house. That was unlike me. I liked being outside. After it all happened, I could hear Connor's country squeaky voice talking as he came up to my house.

He knocks on the door and asks can AJ come outside, ma'am? My mom said just a moment Conor I will ask her. She said AJ, Connor is at the door do you feel like going outside? I said yes mom I will go out for a little while.

He said hey AJ I said hello, Connor. He said he had been to the country with his other grandmother. He said that he missed playing with me. I told him that I could only play at my house. He said, "Okay."

"I got you something AJ." He always called me AJ.

He gave me a racetrack set with cars. I liked racing games. He said he would come back later so we could play.

When he came back to play with me, I was too scared to play with him. His granddad would always watch us. I started telling him I could not play with him anymore because we were moving. I was afraid his granddad would take me away from my family, so I kept telling him that we could not play anymore. I stayed in the house most of the time or I played in the backyard by myself.

I was so afraid of what would happen that I had nightmares,that someone would take me away from my family and hurt me or even kill me. I tried to tell my mom that I had a dream that I was taking away . but she would just say I should pray about it.

How do I tell God something He already knows?

I am nine years old and have been violated but afraid to tell my parents or my siblings what this old white tall slender white man with black hair, grey eyes, did to me. "I quizzed myself on where my dad was? Why didn't he come looking for me." That always played in the back of my mind. A few months later, we did move into a new home and I started to feel happy. It was a new start for me, and I was happy to take it . Even with the fear I had . I was no longer next door Connors grandad the one that hurted me. I was trying to forget everything that had happened to me. I tried to put it all behind me and move onward. I was going to talk to the pastor at the church I was attending, but I heard some people at the church say that you could not tell anyone about what has happened in your life. Half of the time, nobody probably cared anyway. I kept it locked up for years to myself, fighting the hurt and shame of it all. Even though we moved and it felt good not to be watched by a perverted man , I was still watching behind my back my mind was still playing a part in what had happened. Sometimes

I would stay in the house when we first moved there. After some months I stated going outside and meeting some other girls my age.

***

I was coming from a friend's house and I started remembering everything that happened to me almost four years later. I was trying not to think about what happened to me, but out of everything, the sound of that car stood out more than anything else in my mind. But why? I heard a voice say, "You asked for my help and I sent help. The car you heard was sent from me." What? I looked around but no one was there. I said, "Arianna get it together; you hearing things." Then I heard the voice again, and it said, "I sent the car. Arianna, you prayed for me to help you and I did." "God you are talking to me? People said God only speaks to Pastors and Prophets. You are speaking to me, why?" He said it's because I belonged to Him and that He loves me.

Wow, I could not believe that God would speak to someone like me, but I was so grateful that He did. I still had so many unanswered questions, and some questions I didn't even know how to ask.

***

After ruminating down that path again, I came out of it with a banging on my door and my name ringing through, "Arianna, Auntie you okay?"

I snapped, "Yes, yes, I'm okay. I'm up."

I went to the door. It was Karen and Chelsea. They both said, "Are you okay? We have been knocking and beating on your bedroom door."

"I am okay. I was dreaming, but I am fine."

Karen said, "Girl, are you sure you're okay?"

"Yes sweetie, let me shower and I will be downstairs." They sounded all happy.

I said, "Hey, which of y'all is cooking breakfast?"

They yelled back and said, "It's lunch time. We will cook something. We also have some news to tell you."

"Okay, I'll be down shortly." I looked at the time. Wow, it's almost 1pm. I started praying and thanked God for bringing me out with a sound mind and love in my heart. I began to sing: He brought me from a mighty long way. I was so grateful to God, for what He has done and still doing for me and He still speaks to me till this day and He never left me.Even when I was in my mess. Tears rolled down my cheeks as I began to thank Him for beginning so faithful to me when I don't deserve it .

Thank you Jesus.

I went downstairs and the aroma of garlic bread filled the air, yummy. I sat down with Karen and Chelsea while we waited for the other food to finish cooking. They have this big ole grin on their faces. I asked what's going on and how everything is.

Karen said, "Everything is great. Chelsea and I had a long talk about everything, even to when she was younger, and how she felt about her dad's death. Then we talked about what happened with Rodney, and then I got a call from the police station. They said that Rodney will be shipped to Maine. He had warrants for his arrest there, and several other states for molestation, sexual abuse, rape, tickets and other things. So it will be a while before he comes back to this state. I just have to go down and make a statement about when I met him and what happened.

Arianna, Chelsea and I talked for hours. We were up since 4:15am. We talked and cried, forgave each other, then we prayed for forgiveness, we repented unto God. Oh how the love of Jesus came in and sat on us. We were refilled with the Holy Spirit.

God healed us. We realized that it could have been another way, but God said no. You know what Arianna, we even forgave Rodney."

We were in your prayer room when all this took place.

Karen said she feels so free like weights have been lifted off of her. Everything looks so much brighter; she said, "It's something about your prayer room." "It's something about GOD," I said, with tears rolling down my cheeks. It can happen anywhere if you invite the Holy Ghost to come in.

I could feel the unction of the Holy Ghost my God my God. I can't explain it . I was so joyful unto God for healing their relationship and filling them with love for one another and others, for forgiveness, peace and a refilling them with the Holy Ghost. I just thanked God for everything he had done and was doing for them. We were all crying tears of thankfulness. We all realized that it could have been another way. Karen had this scripture for us:

LUKE 8:48 (NIV)

THEN HE SAID TO HER, "DAUGHTER, YOUR FAITH HAS HEALED YOU. GO IN PEACE."

Karen said she had been broken for years, but

was just going on like everything was fine. But everything came out today, and God healed her. We continued in our conversation about how good God is. While we wiped tears away and got ready to eat, Chelsea found pictures of her mom and I when we had a jerry-curl in our hair, back in our elementary days, so we started laughing. While laughing with them, my mind wondered how Rodney could do that and be a youth leader in his church to counsel others. I prayed, "Lord, help the boys and girls he has hurt in any way. Heal them. Only God can heal the heart of every person." Then Karen said to her daughter Chelsae while they were still looking at pictures, Karen came across a picture of us in church. Arianna, do you remember when you first invented me to church? Yep, I sure do. I was 11 years old and you were 12. Karen said you came over to us girls in the neighborhood you came over talking about it's a revival at the church up the street and you would like to invite us to come and go with you. It starts Friday, you said that we could ride with you and your mom. What did they say Auntie Chelsea asked? sweetie they just looked at me like I was speaking a different language. Karen said yeah because we were talking about what boy we liked and then her comes Arianna talking about a church revival really we all started laughing. Sweetie, your mom was one of the ones that used to call me a holy roller. What's that Chelsea asked? Karen said that's when a person goes to church all the time. Chelsea said that should have been a good thing. You would think it would have been," right? But not your mom.

I remember when I was so in love with God. My heart was beating fast and my stomach felt like It was doing summersaults.

I was in love with God . My love for God was so intense, christian television became my norm a commercial came on that said

"Join us for Revival". My eyes lit up like a 100 watt bulb. I could not believe it. A prophet was coming to town. The church was nearby, I ran from the living room to my parents bedroom . I was so excited; I just had to be there " Mom can I go to the revival up the street? My mom said yes I could go and she would go with me. I asked my mom if a few of my friends could go with us? Yes, AJ, only 4 of them can go so they will be comfortable in the car.

I was able to talk to some of my friends to ask their parents permission to go and they could ride with us. Two of my friends went with us. Chelsea your mom was one of them .

***

That night was magical . I could remember it as if it were yesterday. My friends and I sat on the balcony of the church. Every inch of the room was filled with people sitting , standing , and lifting their hands to the ceiling .

The prophet called people out and shared with them what God was saying concerning their life. People were jumping and screaming, as he told them to be healed in the name of Jesus. It was such an experience. I scooted to the edge of my seat. "The Power of God is in this place the Prophet said, he continued with everyone joining hands as he began to pray. People everywhere throughout the church started crying, screaming out , speaking at that time your mom called it gibberish, but it was people speaking in tongues, their heavenly language. People were failing out under the power of the Holy Ghost .

The Prophet kept saying that the Holy Ghost is here.

***

It was indescribable. Even the people on the balcony were falling out and crying. I was captivated by everything that was going on around me, I too found myself yielding to what was taking place . My hands were lifted in the air and I found myself whispering softly ,"Yes, God." I had no idea what I was saying yes to. I just felt that God was talking to me .

I can not explain it , but I knew I wanted to be used by God to help people , Just like how God was using that prophet those nights.

We went back every night and on the last night the prophet asked all the young people to come to the altar, "He instructed us to lift our hands to receive what God has for us. I did not hesitate. I lifted my hands high and waited for my turn to have hands laid on me. While he was praying for other young people, someone was speaking in my ear saying Forgive you have to forgive I began to say that I forgive, and I felt like I had to call out the man's name that hurted me. I said Micheal O'Connor I forgive you, I forgive you. When the prophet came to me he was speaking in tongues. Then he said " Father God, she belongs to you, heal her mind, use her for your Glory God , save now and baptize her with the Holy Ghost and fire!"

In Jesus Name Amen. My Life changed. My hearing was different, My seeing was different. My life changed for the Greater because I had Jesus on the inside of me. Chelsea was crying. She felt the unction(Anointing) of the Holy Ghost in the house with us. Karen started speaking her heavenly language. (speaking in Tongues). Oh my God what a time we had in the house. The present of God was here.

MATTHEW 18:20 (NIV)

For where two or three gather in my name, there am I with them."

***

CHAPTER THREE

THE DAY I STOOD STILL

The day I stood still, and everything that had happened to me when I was a little girl played in my head one after the other, the mortification of it all. All kinds of "whys" invaded my mind, so many unanswered questions. I felt so embarrassed to even face the truth to myself. The thoughts of everything were so painful that I had obliterated them from my mind, at least, I thought I did.

Perturbation played a part in my life for a while. I could hide it well from others, but I could not hide it from God. Self-reproach, regret, blame, low self-worth, culpability, and bewail. I stood still, as I cogitated the things that had taken place when I was younger. It became overwhelming.

I realized I was beating myself up mentally. I realized that I needed and wanted God to heal me, but first I had to acknowledge everything that had happened to me.

As I began to think about these things, I realized that I had to forgive the man that hurt me. How could I do that? Tears rolled down my cheeks because I didn't want to forgive. I was looking for a reason to be angry, to hate. What he did to me, I began to think about Jesus hanging on the cross saying, "ABBA (Father) forgive them for they know not what they do." I cried even the more saying, "God, help me to forgive. I don't want what happened to me to keep me from you, LORD. I want to forgive, help me please."

In my cry and plea for God to help me, He did just that.

I no longer live in that dark place. Everything is bright and beautiful to me now.

JEREMIAH 17:14 (NIV)

Heal me, Lord, and I will be healed; save me and I will be saved, for you are the one I praise.

***

CHAPTER FOUR

POEM
I'M FREE

You looked at me and saw what you wanted,

And you played on the color of my skin to keep me in fear and lock me within,

Always watching behind my back.

All because of what you told me during the attack.

You told me you could get away with it because I was black

You said I was a tasty treat, a fancy feast with everything attached.

I was too developed for my age,

I see, but that doesn't give you permission to

touch me.

You took a chance on my life not knowing if I would get it back,

All because I'm black.

What does the color of my skin have to do with what's within the Blood is still Red at the end?

I'm numb and scared and I am afraid too.

Lord, what should I do?

Who could I tell

What would have happened if I yelled?

I'll never see my family again, oh daddy please help me; don't you hear my cry?

This man said he might kill me and I would die, but something happened.

I could see God sent someone to help me,

a sound I heard a car could it be my mom coming home to rescue me?

I always wonder what I did to deserve this.

I realize it was you with the issue, not me.

I wish I had said something then, maybe, just maybe, my mind may be different within, and got counseling, therapy too, or yelled out for it to end like a book I was reading.

Instead, I held it all within. Depression, anger, and suicide too,

All balled into one what should I do?

Now that years have passed and my life is not the same and things have changed.

I had to break from the hooks and chains that once had me down.

I had to realize you tried to destroy me, crush me and annihilate me,

To keep me wearing a frown.

But I had to forgive you and let you go,

The hurt and the shame, the physical ache, and the emotional pain.

I no longer live in the abyss where you rule and

reign.

I had to be free so I called on Jesus' name,

So I took off the costume of the victim and I put on the garment of victory.

You no longer have power over me. I AM FREE.

The Blood Of Jesus Covers Me.

CHAPTER FIVE

I WILL NOT

- I will not blame myself
- I will not seek revenge
- I will not be bitter
- I will not be fearful
- I will not be silent
- I will not be selfish
- I will not be lonely
- I will not stop dreaming
- I will not hate the one that hurt me
- I will not look down on others
- I will not compare myself to others
- I will not take life for granted
- I will not forget to tell my testimony

I will not forget to enjoy the life God has for me. It was bought with a price by Jesus blood on Calvary

Thank God I'm Free

***

Chapter Six

Encourage yourself with the I AM's.

I AM

- I am Loved by God
- I am never Alone
- I am Loveable
- I am Brave
- I am Beautiful
- I am Unique
- I am Accepted
- I am Protected
- I am Important
- I am Precious

- I am Supportive
- I am Honorable
- I am Empowered
- I am Amazing
- I am Compassionate
- I am Creative
- I am Generous
- I am Faithful
- I am Confident
- I am Chosen
- I am Strong
- I am Positive
- I am Respectful
- I am God's workmanship
- I am seated in heavenly realms
- I am Fearfully and Wonderfully Made by God

***

Have You Been Touched Inappropriately, How Did It Make You Feel And Did You Tell Anyone? How Did You Pray?

_____
_____
_____
_____
_____
_____
_____
_____
_____
_____
_____
_____
_____
_____
_____
_____
_____
_____
_____
_____
_____

Do You Know Anyone That Has Been Touched Inappropriately? If So, How Did You Help Them? How Did You Pray For Them?

BIBLE SCRIPTURES

PSALM 17:8 (NIV)

Keep me as the apple of your eye; hide me in the shadow of your wings

DEUTERONOMY 20:4 (NIV)

For the Lord, your God is he who goes with you to fight for you against your enemies, to give you the victory.

2 CORINTHIANS 12:9-10 (NIV)

But he said to me, "My grace is sufficient for you, for my power is made perfect in weakness." Therefore I will boast all the more gladly of my weaknesses, so that the power of Christ may rest upon me. For the sake of Christ, then, I am content with weaknesses, insults, hardships, persecutions, and calamities. For when I am weak, then I am strong.

JOSHUA 1:9 (ESV)

Have I not commanded you? Be strong and courageous. Do not be frightened, and do not be dismayed, for the Lord your God is with you wherever you go.

COLOSSIANS 3:8 (NKJV)

But now you yourselves are to put off all these: anger, wrath, malice, blasphemy, filthy language out of your mouth.

MATTHEW 18:20-22 (NKJV)

For where two or three are gathered together in My name, I am there in the midst of them.

Then Peter came to Him and said, "Lord, how often shall my brother sin against me, and I forgive him? Up to seven times?"

Jesus said to him, "I do not say to you, up to seven times, but up to seventy times seven.

EPHESIANS 6:10 (ESV)

Finally, be strong in the Lord and in the strength of his might.

PSALM 46:1 (ESV)

God is our refuge and strength, a very present help in trouble.

PSALM 29:11 (ESV)

May the Lord give strength to his people! May the Lord bless his people with peace.

JOHN 16:33 (ESV)

I have said these things to you, that in me you may have peace. In the world, you will have tribulation. But take heart; I have overcome the world.

EPHESIANS 1:4 (NIV)

For he chose us in him before the creation of the world to be holy and blameless in his sight. In love

ROMANS 15:7 (NIV)

Accept one another, then, just as Christ accepted you, in order to bring praise to God.

JOHN 15:10-11 (NIV)

If you keep my commands, you will remain in my love, just as I have kept my Father's commands and remain in his love. 11 I have told you this so that my joy may be in you and that your joy may be complete.

EPHESIANS 6:10 (NIV)

Finally, be strong in the Lord and in his mighty power.

PSALM 16:5 (ERV)

Lord, you give me all that I need.

You support me.

You give me my share.

The Sinner's Prayer

This is a prayer for molesters, sexual abusers, bullies, and anyone that intentionally hurt others in any way.

LUKE 5:32 (NIV)

I have not come to call the righteous, but sinners to repentance".

Father God, I know that I am A sinner and I need a Savior. I want to turn away from my sinful life to the life You have planned for me. Please forgive me for my sins. Cleanse me of my past, make me new. I know Your Son Jesus Christ died for me. I believed in my heart that You raised Him from the dead.

At this very moment, I accept, confess, and

proclaim Jesus Christ as my personal Lord and Savior. To live in my heart from this day forward.

Thank you Jesus for Your Grace and mercy that has saved me from my sins and has given me eternal life. I Receive Your Holy Spirit to guide me and to help me do your will for the rest of my life.

In Jesus name Amen

A Prayer for You

Father God, In the name of Jesus, we thank you now for your love and kindness. We thank you for your tender mercies. Father, we thank you for being in control of everything. We bind the hands, feet, and mouth of Satan and his army that tries to come against my mind, emotions, to blame me for the molestation that was done to me.

Father, we bind up fears in our relationships to trust people and our love for people. We plead the Blood of Jesus Christ is upon our minds now. We bind up all the different evil spirits now, and we call them out in the name of Jesus. Self-blame, revenge, worry, fear, depression, anger, loneliness, humiliation, confusion, helplessness, irritation, disappointment, doubtful, discouragement, worthlessness, bitterness, uncertainty, paralyzed, shame, frustrated, powerless, perplexed, useless, guilt, emptiness, shyness, vulnerable, offensive, hesitant, unbelieving, resentful, and unforgiveness

Father God, we loose the Love of Jesus Christ and Your Peace; and call healing now in the name of Jesus.

We lose knowledge, wisdom, greatness, loving, confidence, peace, joy, energetic, abundance, amazement, fortunate, delightful, encouraged, thankful, kind, cheerful, bright, blessed, merry, strong, satisfied, boldness, passionate, highly favored also Forgiveness for yourself and others.

Rejoice because GOD is restoring you, making you whole again.

You are not a Victim, but you are Victorious.

May GOD be with you, keep you and bless you

In Jesus' name Amen.

ABOUT THE AUTHOR

Pamela Tucker is an advocate for the forgotten. Her heart for people and efforts to help others live their best lives has made her an active humanitarian.

She has three daughters and one granddaughter.

Pamela is the author of:

- Forgive Me Forgive Me Not Vol 1, 2, 3, 4.
- Why Are You Broke When You Say You Know Jesus?
- It's Nothing But Gibberish.

Pamela Tucker resides in metro Atlanta where she lives a life of Forgiveness.

www.ingramcontent.com/pod-product-compliance
Lightning Source LLC
Chambersburg PA
CBHW020958090426
42736CB00010B/1378